GHOSTS IN THE COTTONWOODS

Adam Rapp

BROADWAY PLAY PUBLISHING INC
New York
www.broadwayplaypublishing.com
info@broadwayplaypublishing.com

GHOSTS IN THE COTTONWOODS
© Copyright 2014 by Adam Rapp

Cover photo by Annie Parisse
First printing: June 2014
I S B N: 978-0-88145-543-4
Book design: Marie Donovan
Page make-up: Adobe Indesign
Typeface: Palatino
Printed and bound in the U S A

GHOSTS IN THE COTTONWOODS received a
workshop production at the 1996 National Playwrights
Conference (Lloyd Richards Artistic Director) in
Waterford, CT. The cast and creative contributor were:

BEAN SCULLY .... Maryann Plunkett
POINTER SCULLY ....Paul McCrane
NEWT YARDLY ....John Bedford Lloyd
SHIRLEY JUDYHOUSE................................. Katherine Hiler
JEFFCAT SCULLY ....Timothy Devlin

Director .... Amy Saltz

The world premiere of GHOSTS IN THE COTTONWOODS was produced by The Rivendell Theatre Ensemble at Victory Gardens in Chicago. Opening Night was November 24th, 1998 with the following cast:

BEAN SCULLY ....Peggy Dunne
POINTER SCULLY .... George McConnell
NEWT YARDLY ....Nathan Rankin
SHIRLEY JUDYHOUSE................................... Callie Beaulieu
JEFFCAT SCULLY ....Shannon Parr

Director ....Jeremy Cohen

The Off-Broadway premiere of GHOSTS IN THE COTTONWOODS was produced by The Amoralists Theatre Company at Theatre 80 Saint Mark's in New York City's East Village. Opening night was 16 November 2010. The cast and creative contribors were as follows:

BEAN SCULLY	Sarah Lemp
POINTER SCULLY	Nick Lawson
NEWT YARDLY	William Apps
SHIRLEY JUDYHOUSE	Mandy Nicole Moore
JEFF SCULLY	James Kautz
GORDON	Matthew Pilieci
Director	Adam Rapp
Set design	Alfred Schatz
Lights	Keith Parham
Sound	Eric Shimelonis
Costumes	Jessica Pabst

This version of the play was radically rewritten and re-imagined, and all changes are reflected in this edition.

CHARACTERS & SETTING

POINTER SCULLY, 20, *Caucasian, feral, hopeful*
BEAN SCULLY, 36, POINTER'*s mother*
NEWT, 40, *a charmer*
SHIRLEY JUDYHOUSE, 20, POINTER'*s girlfriend, a dreamer*
JEFF SCULLY, 22, POINTER'*s brother, almost an animal*
GORDON, *ageless,* JEFF'*s friend from prison, savage*

Time: the night of a terrible storm

Place: Nowhere and anywhere

(The sound of wind and rain)

(The interior of a homemade house. A strange hodgepodge of tarpaper, floorboards, corrugated metal, fence planking, particleboard, old tabletops, etc. No furniture, except for an enormous table that perhaps looks as if it was at one time a door, and a few orphaned and makeshift chairs. The table is fully dressed with three settings. Somewhere over the table, perhaps hanging on a nail, an old bowler hat. Candles are lit. A few lanterns as well. A makeshift kitchen area. No sink. A basin without plumbing. A mini-stovetop. Food has been prepared in heaping bowls. There is a large pitcher of lemonade centered on the table. Also present downstage right is a dynamo wheel that has been somehow fashioned to a generator: the small house's sole source of electricity.)

(There is a window upstage left whose appearance should suggest that it has been somehow scavenged. There is a single entrance, upstage center-right. Stage left, an enormous, coiled tugboat rope is cranked on an old fire-hose wheel.)

(Downstage left is the rusted back end of a small sports car, its trunk serving as a storage space. Or maybe a footlocker.)

(A hip-hop outfit is strewn over the back of one chairs, a pair of cheap hiking boots [imitation Timberlands] underneath the chair. A baseball hat with a flattened bill.)

(A drain downstage center. POINTER SCULLY stands naked in front of the drain. His head is crudely shaved. There are red welts all over his body. BEAN SCULLY, his mother, is knelt at his side, dressed in a homemade dress. Her hair is up. There is an old paint can set at her side. She is sucking *on one of the welts on* POINTER's *outstretched arms. He speaks with a slight stutter.)*

BEAN: *(Spitting into the paint can)* You plant the rifle?

POINTER: I planted it.

BEAN: Thirty-aught-six or the flintlock?

POINTER: Both.

BEAN: You load em?

POINTER: Course I loaded em.

BEAN: Extra shells?

POINTER: Entire box each.

BEAN: *(Spitting)* What in God's name are you so nervous about?

POINTER: All types of stuff in them woods.

*(*BEAN *sucks on a welt between* POINTER's *shoulder blades)*

POINTER: Hackbores. Slownecks. Crazy things. The Flaptooth.

BEAN: Ain't nary a flaptooth in them woods.

POINTER: Dogsnakes, too.

BEAN: Pointer, ain't nary a flaptooth and ain't nary a dogsnake in them woods. That's crazy.

POINTER: How do you know? You don't go out there. Stuff evolves.

BEAN: Bend over.

*(*POINTER *does so.)*

POINTER: Comes right up out of the water. Fish turn into squirrels. Squirrels turn into snakes. Stuff evolves like that. Especially when it rains. I seen what frogs do. The way they change. I seen it.

*(*BEAN *slaps* POINTER's *butt and he stands up again.)*

BEAN: Everything changes, Pointer.

POINTER: Not like no frogs. Their tails fall off. Their throats puff up. They make noises. I hear em in the trees. And they don't sound like frogs is supposed to sound. Sound more like hogs gruntin.

(BEAN *finishes with his sores.* POINTER *starts to dress: baggy basketball shorts, a T-shirt three sizes too large, the cheap hiking boots, the baseball cap.*)

BEAN: You been spendin too much time in that fishpond.

POINTER: Ain't nothin wrong with that fishpond.

BEAN: That's how come all them leeches got to ya. Them leeches'll suck the sap right outta your blood and the sense right outta your head.

POINTER: He prolly ain't even gonna show.

BEAN: Pointer, he is comin and I can feel it! He's prolly rippin through them woods as we speak! …My burners are going cold, I need you to ride.

(POINTER *goes to his knees, mans the dynamo wheel, pedals it with his hands. After a moment, he sticks his hand down his shorts, scratches his crotch.*)

BEAN: Stop that!

POINTER: It itches.

BEAN: Good Godfrey! Get your hand out your drawers!

(POINTER *removes his hand, smells it.*)

BEAN: I told you to stop fussin with that johnson grass. If the good lord wanted it in your drawers he wouldn't grow it outta the ground.

POINTER: I ain't been fussin with no johnson grass.

BEAN: Every time I warsh your damn clothes I find it. Nothin but johnson grass.

(POINTER *continues pedaling the dynamo wheel.*)

BEAN: That's enough ridin. *(Referring to the paint can)* Empty that for me please.

(POINTER stops riding, moves away the dynamo wheel, grabs the paint can, empties it down the drain.)

BEAN: You got his present ready?

POINTER: Yeah.

BEAN: I hope you been keepin it right. Ort to not look sickly.

POINTER: *(Mocking her)* Ort to not look sickly. *(He "orts" like a sow several times, then mumbles something, crosses to the window.)*

BEAN: Mumbler… Just make sure you have it ready when he walks through that door. It's been six years and he *ort* to feel missed.

POINTER: *(At the window)* Can't even see no glowbugs.

BEAN: Ain't seen nary a glowbug in a dog's age.

POINTER: Saw some last night.

BEAN: Where?

POINTER: Over by the fishpond. They was doin somersaults.

BEAN: Fishpond, fishpond, Pointer and his fishpond.

POINTER: I caught one and put it in a Coke bottle.

BEAN: Who's in the fishpond? *Pointer's* in the fishpond.

POINTER: Caught it with my bare hand. Little sucker was glowin like Christmas. *(Looking out the front door)* Can't see them lanterns.

BEAN: He's prolly blowin em out like he's sposed to.

POINTER: No glowbugs. No lanterns. It don't make no damn sense, do it?

BEAN: *You* don't make no damn sense.

POINTER: You don't make no damn sense nuther.

BEAN: You look like a freaky deaky.

POINTER: *You* look like a freaky deaky.

BEAN: You look like something that fell off the crazy truck. Egg-headed nimwit.

POINTER: Girls like my head.

BEAN: What girls.

POINTER: Just girls in general.

BEAN: The ones who are generally creepy.

POINTER: Shows what you know.

BEAN: I can't imagine a blind whore with nary a tooth likin that head of yours.

POINTER: Well maybe you should talk to the Judyhouse Sisters.

BEAN: The *Judyhouse sisters*!

POINTER: Damn skippy.

BEAN: I spose you think they fancy your head.

POINTER: I know they do.

BEAN: Yeah, you know like a crow and that ain't much.

POINTER: I know what I know, I just go with the flow.

BEAN: You think you're slick.

POINTER: That's right, I'm Slick Rick on the re-quest line I'd like to know your name and your zodiac sign.

BEAN: Good Godfrey.

POINTER: They tried to taste it.

BEAN: *Taste* it?

POINTER: Yum-yum delicious. They tried to lick it.

BEAN: Lick what?

POINTER: My head.

BEAN: *Who?*

POINTER: The Judyhouse sisters.

BEAN: Which one?

POINTER: *All* of em.

BEAN: Oh that's the craziest thing I heard in about four damn days.

POINTER: Believe what you will.

BEAN: Why on God's greasy earth would they want to lick your head?

POINTER: Shirley Judyhouse said it was shapely.

BEAN: Shapely?! That's hog gravy!

POINTER: It's what she said.

BEAN: …Did you let em?

POINTER: Let em what?

BEAN: LICK. YOUR. HEAD.

POINTER: I don't gotta answer that.

BEAN: Yes you do.

POINTER: How so?

BEAN: Cause I'm your Momma, that's how so! And if I wanna make you grow your hair back, I'll do it, Mister *Shapely!* You'll stay in this house and grow it out till it's down to your shoulders! …So?

POINTER: So what?

BEAN: DID THEY LICK YOUR HEAD?

POINTER: Yes.

BEAN: Oh that is so foul.

POINTER: I liked it.

BEAN: Absolutely foul.

POINTER: I liked it a lot, actually.

BEAN: God knows you did.

POINTER: Felt like somethin that might happen in a movie, I'll tell you that right now.

BEAN: Oh I'm sure it did. Foolish old fool. What a story.

POINTER: Stories are for children and I ain't no child.

BEAN: …How old is that Judyhouse girl anyways?

POINTER: *(Mockingly)* Which one?

BEAN: SHIRLEY.

POINTER: Sixteen, seventeen. Why?

BEAN: Looks more like a rock to me. Or a bowling pin. *Shapely*, lord.

POINTER: *(Proudly)* Judyhouse girls rolled up on me right outside that gas station on Fish Street! All six of em! And then Shirley Judyhouse gave me a Jay-Z cassette and lined her sisters up shortest to tallest. Then they started rollin their tongues around inside their mouths like they had gum. And one by one they stepped up to the love zone like a buncha starved alleycats: Elsa Judyhouse, Lynne-Lynne Judyhouse, Recita Judyhouse, Katie Judyhouse, Shirley Judyhouse, and Billie Jean King Judyhouse.

BEAN: Billie Jean King Judyhouse?

POINTER: Billie Jean King Judyhouse.

(BEAN and POINTER repeat "Billy Jean King Judyhouse" back and forth several times. Then:)

POINTER: Afterwards I felt so damn special I came close to makin a speech.

BEAN: A *speech*? What kinda speech?

POINTER: I don't know. Prolly woulda let flow some lyrics or somethin.

BEAN: *Lyrics?*

POINTER: *(Proudly)* "Hot foot showdown/lookin for a throwdown/don't believe that burger/he from the nowhere no town."

BEAN: You're gettin stranger and stranger every day, Pointer. It's startin to scare me. Your crazy head. Them awful clothes.

POINTER: I like my clothes. I feel like a sex maniac in these clothes.

BEAN: You're too young to feel like a sex maniac.

POINTER: You wrong as a song that's twelve minutes long.

BEAN: The things you say.

POINTER: I got twenty years under my belt! I feel sexy as a damn horse on derby day!

BEAN: You know nary a thing about sexy.

POINTER: I'll go get my radio right now and I'll throw on some Nas. Or some Poor Righteous Teachers. And I'll rock this funky joint right here in the Life Room. I'll show you sexy.

BEAN: You will do nary the thing in my Life Room.

POINTER: I'll pull out my Casablanca light, too, Momma. I swear to Sunday Jesus.

BEAN: *(Severe)* You bring any of that hog gravy into my Life Room and I'll have you outta this house so fast you'll be whittlin sticks, you understand me boy!? I will not have that hammisexual nigra music in my house. That music's bendin your mind in all the wrong ways.

POINTER: Tasseled corn all summer for that radio.

BEAN: Them baggie clothes.

POINTER: This is the style! You just don't know! I earned these shorts. *And* this shirt. *And* these tims. *And* this fresh-ass lid. Just like I earned my radio… You don't know what it's like out there fieldwalkin no more. Corn taller than you are. Can't see no sky. Your arms start itchin. Your mind starts wanderin. All them rows.

BEAN: And your hat's too damn big.

POINTER: Big as in amazin.

BEAN: Always wearin that big dopey hat. Never saw a person iron the bill of a hat afore. Straight from the Devil's cupboard.

POINTER: You just don't know about that stuff.

BEAN: You keep wearin that dopey hat like that and you're liable to confuse your brain.

POINTER: My brain's just fine, but I appreciate the concern.

BEAN: I spose Shirley Judyhouse likes them baggy clothes, too.

POINTER: She never said nothin about em.

BEAN: She'd prolly like to lick them shorts.

POINTER: Never said nothin about these shorts.

BEAN: Your brother ain't fulla calamity and wickedness.

POINTER: Yeah, well some dogs'll chase themselves straight into a hole if you put enough gravy on their tail.

(Beat)

BEAN: Pour me a drink.

POINTER: *(Under his breath)* Pour your own drink, dummy.

(BEAN *shoots* POINTER *a deadly stare. He submits, finds an an old oil can, pours her a glass of whiskey.*)

BEAN: Go get me my cigarettes.

(POINTER *crosses back to the car trunk, roots through it again, and returns with a pack of cigarettes. He sets them down in front of her with a box of matches.* BEAN *throws the matches across the room.*)

BEAN: Light me.

(POINTER *does so.*)

BEAN: Tuck your shirt in.

(POINTER *tucks in his shirt and crosses to matches, retrieves them, crosses back to* BEAN, *and lights her cigarette. She takes a long drag, blows it out the side of her mouth and takes a large gulp of whiskey. He crosses to the downstage left corner, sits.*)

POINTER: You smoke like a man. Like you pump gas or somethin.

BEAN: Your daddy and I used to roll our own cigarettes. He had them tricky thumbs. Could do two at one time…I tried to get your brother to start smokin but he wouldn't touch it.

POINTER: Jeff ain't no smoker.

BEAN: No he ain't. And you ain't nuther.

POINTER: Ain't good for you.

BEAN: Oh that's hog gravy.

POINTER: Makes your heart turn black.

BEAN: Anything can turn your heart black, Pointer. Anything in this world.

POINTER: And you ain't supposed to have no babies if you smoke.

BEAN: You and your brother came out just fine.

POINTER: We got lucky. If you smoke too much they'll shrivel up and fall out.

BEAN: Who's fillin your head with these crazy notions?

POINTER: Ain't no one's fillin my head with nothin, nigga! That's just stuff you know about.

BEAN: It ain't just stuff you know about, Pointer… Sneakin around behind my back.
Smoke with me, Pointer.

POINTER: No ma'am.

BEAN: C'mon, blow on a ciggy with your Mommalove.

POINTER: You gotta have lung strength to be a hip-hop star, Momma! How am I sposed to keep my lung strength if I start smokin?

BEAN: Just this once.

POINTER: No ma'am. I'm in trainin. Jay-Z ain't no smoker. Nor is Fitty-cent. They got lung strength.

BEAN: How do you know? We ain't got nary a T V. And I know you ain't been to no movie house.

POINTER: From magazines.

BEAN: Magazines lie.

POINTER: Not *The Source*, Momma. Not that magazine. That's the leading hip-hop magazine in the world. They got pitchers of all these freestylers like Charron and the Surgeon General battling in New York City. Right in the middle of this big-ass basement they can't even name cause it's like illegal. It's right there in the magazine.

BEAN: Some dream: to wind up in some basement in New York City. You'll prolly get murdered.

POINTER: *(Quietly)* Well then we'll have somethin that runs in the family.

(BEAN throws her drink.)

(Both look at the empty glass for a moment. POINTER *walks over to the table and refills it for her. A cold stare from* BEAN. *He moves away from her. After a brief pause:)*

POINTER: Someday I'ma go there. I'ma get my rhymes right and I'ma get my lung strength up and I'ma go right to that basement and get my pitcher in that magazine.

BEAN: If you smoke with me I'll listen to some of your lyrics.

POINTER: You won't.

BEAN: I promise I will. I know you been workin on somethin.

POINTER: You said stuff like that before.

BEAN: But tonight is special.

POINTER: Six years is a long time, ain't it? I was still little when he left.

BEAN: He's prolly gonna be real happy to see you.

POINTER: You think?

BEAN: Of course. He's your only brother. Go on… Go fetch your radio.

*(*POINTER *scurries under the table, pulling aside makeshift curtains, closing them behind him.)*

*(*BEAN *takes a drink of whiskey. The sounds of wind and rain can be heard outside.)*

*(*POINTER *emerges from under the table with a small, dilapidated cassette player, sets it down.)*

POINTER: You really gonna let me rhyme after we smoke?

BEAN: I promise… If you dance with me.

POINTER: I'll dance with your skinny-ass.

(POINTER *approaches* BEAN *slowly and she offers him a lit cigarette. He inhales smoothly. She takes his cigarette, smokes. He presses play on the cassette player. The Poor Righteous Teachers' "Rock This Funky Joint" plays at a low volume)*

(BEAN *takes his hand. They dance.* POINTER *tries to dance in a way he's seen on videos. He raps along, mouthing the words. She indulges him for a moment and then calms him and it turns into a slow dance.)*

POINTER: *(While dancing)* He wrote to me, Momma. He told me some stuff they done to him at Shiloh. How they got little kids mixed up with old men. How some folks get treated… He wrote how this man with no jaw strapped him to his bunk with belts and lined up a bunch of little boys and had them toss off directly on him. Said the man had some kind of whippin wire. Jeff said he had to sleep in their dogwater. That ain't right, Momma. I'll kill that jawless bastard.

(BEAN *and* POINTER *dance.)*

BEAN: You keep growin and growin, Pointer. You're gonna be tall as a pole afore it's all over… Somethin about them Scully bones. Both my boys got such crazy bones… Your daddy used to let me stand on his boots when we'd dance. *(She steps onto his Timberlands.)* Afore you boys was born we'd slow-step it for hours. Uncle Drexel would come over with his banjo and set in the Barcelona Chair and sing Curly Bluejack. Uncle Drexel had a history in his voice…I'd be right up on his boots…like I was floatin.

(BEAN *puts her hands on his face, looks intently into his eyes. He places his hands over hers. It starts to thunder. Lightning flashes out the window. A loud gunshot is heard.)*

POINTER: What was that?

BEAN: Lightnin.

POINTER: Funny soundin lightnin.

BEAN: Just saw it flash out the window.

(BEAN *and* POINTER *continue to dance.*)

BEAN: Who's tellin you stuff about babies, Pointer? It ain't the tinker is it?

POINTER: No.

BEAN: Jeff ain't tellin you nothin in them letters is he?

POINTER: Just what I told you.

BEAN: Is it Shirley Judyhouse?

(POINTER *doesn't answer.* BEAN *stops dancing.*)

BEAN: It's that little twelve cent hussy, ain't it!?

(POINTER *bows his head, ashamed.*)

BEAN: …Answer me you sinful little dog!

(BEAN *slaps* POINTER *and he falls to his knees and holds his face.*)

BEAN: Get to the chair!

(POINTER *goes to the chair and prepares for his punishment.* BEAN *stops the cassette player, approaches him wielding a hot skillet, poised to strike.*)

(*A knock at the door*)

(BEAN *stops.* POINTER *escapes under the table with his cassette player. She returns the skillet to the stovetop. Another knock*)

BEAN: Jeff?

(*Pounding on the door*)

NEWT: (*Off*) Help me! Somebody! God Christ! I need help!

(*More pounding*)

NEWT: (*Off*) Can somebody help me please?

(BEAN *opens the front door.* NEWT *stands in the entrance, hopping on one leg, clutching his knee with both hands. Blood has soaked through his blue jeans. He is drenched.*)

BEAN: Dear Jesus!

NEWT: Just help me set! Please!

(BEAN *helps the* MAN *sit, props his leg on another chair. He screams in pain.* POINTER *scurries out the door, from under the table, unseen.*)

BEAN: Pointer get in here! This man's hurt! We gotta get help!

NEWT: Just get me a splint! And some rope! A splint and some rope! I think my leg's busted!… Some whiskey. Whatever you got. Please.

(BEAN *sets her oil can before him, crosses to the car trunk, starts to root through it.* NEWT *takes a long chug, wipes his mouth, exhales. He takes another long chug. She crosses to him with a broken broomstick and a length of rope.*)

NEWT: I need somethin to cut the rope with. A buck knife! I need a buck knife!

(BEAN *produces a buck knife.* NEWT *cuts the rope into two sections and ties it around the broomstick, which he uses as a splint.*)

BEAN: What the devil happened?

NEWT: Some crazy sumbuck shot me!

BEAN: Where?

NEWT: Woods!

BEAN: Good Godfrey.

NEWT: He was settin in a tree!

BEAN: You poor unfortunate man.

NEWT: Biggest oak I ever saw in my life. He was settin in it. It was hollow.

BEAN: What on earth was you doin in them woods at this hour?

NEWT: *(Struggling)* My truck clutched up on me bout a mile and a half from here. Radiator. I was takin a short cut. And someone just hauls off and unloads on me. Thirty-aught-six. I'm lucky it hit a tree first or it woulda blown my leg clear off.

BEAN: You sure it was a thirty-aught-six?

NEWT: Ma'am, I know guns like a dog knows Gravy Train.

BEAN: Pointer!

NEWT: Ma'am please! I just need to rest. I'll be fine. Besides, it's stormin like crazy out there.

(Lightning flashes in the window.)

BEAN: It'll get infested. Germs and such. Rotleg. It'll get infested and then it'll fall off.

NEWT: I'll just pour some whiskey on it.

BEAN: It'll fall on the floor and someone'll steal it!

NEWT: I promise you that ain't gonna happen.

BEAN: POINTER, GET YOUR SKINNY BEHIND IN HERE!

(NEWT pours whiskey over the wound. He grimaces, his body contorting with pain. He falls to the floor. BEAN quickly crosses to him, helps him back into the chair.)

BEAN: Jesus Christmas on a stick!

NEWT: *(In pain)* Knew a fella once who got shot in the stomach. Sprained both ankles, lost his two front teeth, threw his knee out, and made it home in time for chow. Lived to be damn near eighty. Said keepin his guts in was the tough stuff. Had to use fishin line. His wife pulled the bullet out with her bare hands. Lived to be damn near eighty.

BEAN: Well, I ain't no nursemaid. Pointer!

NEWT: Please, just stay here till I get my bearings…
You don't got no phone do you?

BEAN: No sir, I'm afraid I don't.

NEWT: No ceebee radio or nothin, huh?

BEAN: All I got is a loud voice. And I'm afraid my voice
can't compete with that wind.

(NEWT *vomits on the floor.* BEAN *crosses to clean the mess
with a rag. Then:)*

NEWT: Sorry. *(After a beat)* What's that?

BEAN: Oh, that's the Sodabush Rope.

NEWT: Sodabush?

BEAN: *(Cleaning the vomit with a rag)* That's right.

NEWT: What's it for?

BEAN: Mudslops. Keeps the house in one spot. We
throw it over the Jerry Stump when the hill starts
slidin.

NEWT: Jerry Stump?

BEAN: It's out back.

NEWT: Huh. You get a lotta them round here?

BEAN: Jerry Stumps?

NEWT: No, mudslops.

BEAN: Bout four times a year. You know they're comin
cause the bushchickens start walkin backwards. Like
they forgot somethin.

NEWT: Have you all *slid* before.

BEAN: About forty clicks since the house was built.
Two years ago we had a twelve click troublejump. Lost
the thump hitch and half the stompinporch. We used
to live up by the crazy stone.

NEWT: Well, I'm glad you all finally came to rest.

(BEAN *throws the soiled rag in the trash.*)

BEAN: You gotta have weight in a house to keep it from slidin. Round here stuff'll keep right on rollin if you don't snatch on to somethin.

NEWT: Gravity's a tricky old dog.

BEAN: Sodabush Rope helps a lot. We ain't moved nary a click since we got it.

NEWT: Why you call it that?

BEAN: Cause of the sodabushes. Them low beardly lookin shrubs at the bottom of the slippin zone. Did it look like things were startin to slip out there? You didn't see no trees runnin did you?

NEWT: Can't say I did.

BEAN: Cause when the mudslop gets goin they'll run down a hill. Saw one on fire once. Lookeded like a man fleeskitterin from Hell.

NEWT: Maybe you should rope us in just in case.

BEAN: Oh we have a stretch or two yet. Them bushchickens get to goin backwards and I'll get us hitched in.

NEWT: What's your name?

BEAN: Rayanne. But you can call me Bean.

NEWT: Bean?

BEAN: Yessir.

NEWT: Like snap bean?

BEAN: That's right. Bean Scully. What's yours?

NEWT: Newt.

BEAN: Newt?

NEWT: That's right. Newt. Rhymes with boot.

BEAN: Or root.

NEWT: Parachute.

BEAN: Um...

NEWT: *(Quickly)* Chinese flute. Store fulla loot.

BEAN: Oh, I like word games!

NEWT: Newton Yardly.

(BEAN and NEWT share laughter.)

BEAN: You ain't from around here, are you, Newton Yardly?

NEWT: I ain't been into these parts in over fourteen years.

BEAN: Where you from?

NEWT: Further North. Jackson County.

BEAN: Ain't never been up there.

NEWT: Good fishin up there. Got trout the size of Toyotas. *(He suddenly grabs his leg in pain.)*

BEAN: You gotta stop talkin. You ain't gonna have no lung strength left.

NEWT: Oh, I been shot before. Twice in the hip and once through my hand. *(He holds his hand up.)*

NEWT: It's a strange thing, gettin shot. You'd think it happens like it does on T V. Fellas clutchin their chests and fallin on top of birthday cakes and all that.

BEAN: We don't got no T V.

NEWT: Takin eight-nine rounds in the gut and still professin their love in

the middle of a stampede.

BEAN: Tried to buy a T V once but there was too much voltage. Woulda set the house on fire.

NEWT: Gettin shot ain't nothin like that. Nothin like that at all. *(He drinks heavily.)*

NEWT: Good batch of whiskey you got here. Brewed it up yourself, I bet.

BEAN: That's right.

NEWT: Tastes like homebrew... Thing about gettin shot is *(He drinks.)* that you feel it before you hear it. Bullet travels faster than the speed of sound. It's kinda like aftertaste. But with guns.

BEAN: Bet it hurts.

NEWT: Hurts your whole body. When I got clipped in the hand the pain shot clear through my tailbone.

BEAN: Can't imagine it.

NEWT: Straight through. Felt like gettin struck by lightnin.

BEAN: You been struck by lightnin?

NEWT: Four times.

BEAN: Four times!

NEWT: That's right. I try not to wear nothin metal no more.

BEAN: Dear Jesus.

NEWT: Don't carry no change in my pockets neither.

BEAN: Good strategy.

NEWT: Prolly won't happen again. I'd like to think that Mother Nature's done crapped out on me.

BEAN: Mother Nature's got crazy ideas for folks.

NEWT: You tend to gravitate toward superstition after she's had her way with you a few times.

(The downstage drain gurgles. BEAN crosses to it, discretely covers it with a small rug.)

(Beat)

BEAN: So what was you doin in these parts fourteen years ago?

NEWT: I was lookin for someone.

BEAN: You lost a friend?

NEWT: No. I was tryin to find this fella who was fond of swingsets.

BEAN: Swingsets?

NEWT: He loved swingsets. I think they were his favorite thing.

BEAN: Did you ever find him?

NEWT: No. They say he disappeared.

BEAN: What was you gonna do if you found him?

NEWT: I was just gonna talk to him.

BEAN: He needed a talkin to?

NEWT: Yeah, he needed a talkin to. He needed someone to take his swingsets away. *(He drinks.)*

NEWT: You got any needle and thread?

BEAN: I believe so.

NEWT: I think I better close this up. I'm bleedin like a sieve.

(BEAN opens some drawer, starts rooting through it. NEWT quickly removes a cellphone from an interior jacket pocket, checks it for service, shakes his head, hides it. She closes the drawer, crosses to him with a spool of thread and a needle, the needle already threaded.)

NEWT: You got nothin but black thread, huh?

BEAN: Had some blue but I used it up on patches.

NEWT: You don't got no white?

BEAN: Nosir.

NEWT: Black'll make me look all mangled.

BEAN: Sorry.

(NEWT *uses a lighter to burn the head of the needle, burns his wound with it as well.*)

BEAN: What about the bullet? …You ort to take it out. I got a fork if you need it.

NEWT: Ain't nothin in there. That slug passed directly through me. (*He takes another large swig from the whiskey, wipes his mouth, starts sewing his leg shut, grimacing.*)

BEAN: (*Still standing over him*) Don't that hurt?

NEWT: Course it hurts.

BEAN: You ain't hollerin or nothin.

NEWT: That's cause I'm two-thirds in shock.

BEAN: Oh. How does it feel?

NEWT: My leg?

BEAN: No, shock.

NEWT: It ain't no carnival.

BEAN: I admire your tolerance.

NEWT: I couldn't trouble you for an extra blanket, could I? Somethin to throw over my shoulders.

(BEAN *nods, disappears under the table returns with* POINTER's *blanket, hands it to* NEWT, *who sets it down next to his chair.*)

NEWT: (*Still sewing*) Looks like you were fixin to have some kinda special dinner here tonight.

BEAN: Yeah. I cooked up some chuck steak.

NEWT: Fine lookin vittles. What's the occasion?

BEAN: My oldest boy is comin home.

NEWT: That right?

BEAN: Yessir. Shoulda been here by now.

NEWT: Awful late for a home comin.

BEAN: He had to travel at night.

NEWT: Well I apologize for any inconvenience.

BEAN: Aw slaw, you ain't inconveniencin nothin.

NEWT: You got two boys?

BEAN: Yessir.

NEWT: They help you round here, I reckon.

BEAN: Well, only one of em's been round lately. Older one's been upstate for a while.

NEWT: How long?

BEAN: Oh, a dog's age. Six years, actually.

NEWT: Pretty long stretcha time.

BEAN: Things change a lot in six years.

NEWT: He ain't been harvestin crops, I gather.

BEAN: Naw, he's just been upstate… He's gonna be so thrilled to be home.

NEWT: I bet.

BEAN: I bet he'll cry.

NEWT: Ain't nothin wrong with that.

BEAN: Well, he ort to. I'll prolly have to fetch him a rag or somethin.

NEWT: *(Offering the spool of thread and needle)* You mind?

(BEAN accepts the needle and thread, rethreads the needle, hands it back. This may take a moment. NEWT falls into her a bit. He might even sing a song to keep himself focused away from the pain. His singing is barely audible. When she is successful threading the needle, she hands it back to him.)

NEWT: You ain't married, are you?

BEAN: Used to be.

NEWT: He skedaddled on you?

BEAN: He died.

NEWT: What was his name?

BEAN: Walter…Walter MacMurray Scully… *(Looking at the bowler hat on the wall)* That was his hat.

(NEWT looks at the hat. BEAN watches NEWT. After a moment:)

NEWT: Why you lookin at me like that?

BEAN: Somethin you just did reminded me of him.

NEWT: What'd I do?

BEAN: I don't know… What'd you do?

(Beat)

NEWT: I hear about how folks get sick a lot in these parts. Night fevers and such.

BEAN: Oh he didn't get sick. He was healthy as a duck. He fell down a hole.

NEWT: A sink hole?

BEAN: No, just a hole. Fell down it and never came back up.

(NEWT continues to sew his leg.)

BEAN: You ain't married nuther.

NEWT: No ma'am, I ain't. My line of work ain't too easy on a filly.

BEAN: What line of work you in?

NEWT: I'm a collector.

BEAN: A collector?

NEWT: That's right.

BEAN: Jeejoos and such?

NEWT: Jeejoos?

BEAN: Snagtags, flickerdills, yucktimmytoos.

NEWT: Debts.

BEAN: Oh. You a repo man.

NEWT: Sort of.

BEAN: That's why you got a truck. So you can haul swingsets and such. *(Pause)* They came and took the Barcelona chair a coupla months ago.

NEWT: I seen one of them once.

BEAN: Only nice thing we had.

NEWT: Barcelona chair.

BEAN: It's great for pickin a banjo cause it don't got no arms.

NEWT: Tough line of work.

BEAN: Can't imagine it bein too friendly.

NEWT: You have your days.

BEAN: That's prolly how you got shot all them times. Coupla them bad days.

(NEWT finishes sewing.)

NEWT: All done. *(Flaunting his work)* Shoulda been a dressmaker.

(BEAN and NEWT laugh. The laughter dies.)

NEWT: Where do you sleep around here?

BEAN: Over there.

(BEAN and NEWT look at the downstage left nest area.)

BEAN: Under here's my son's room.

(BEAN pulls aside the table-curtain, revealing POINTER's private little room. A lava lamp, magazines, a diminutive bed. They look. She closes the curtain.)

BEAN: Do you need to lay down?

NEWT: No, I was just…

(In the distance, an odd whistling sound. Is it a bird? A man?)

(Beat)

NEWT: Food gettin cold?

BEAN: I cooked it up hot. A special kinda hot so it won't get cold till later. Jeff loves chuck steak. That boy can put away a flanka chuck steak like nobody's business… Six years is a dog's age.
Wonder what he looks like now. Cause a face'll change on you. The nose stretches. The eyes get smaller. The hair grows wild. That's what happens.

NEWT: I reckon you're right.

BEAN: Those bones'll shift up and fool you…I'll bet he turned out tall.
And strong as a bull.

NEWT: He prolly did, Bean. Prolly did…

BEAN: You like Curly Bluejack?

NEWT: Can't say I hearda him.

BEAN: Used to sing on top of Jumblestick Hill. Carried a duck wherever he went. Some folks say he was married to it just like a woman.

NEWT: Sounds like an interstin fella.

BEAN: Could make his voice sound like a goatdog buckin at the moon.

NEWT: You familiar with Merle Haggard?

BEAN: Is that a furniture store?

NEWT: *(Laughing)* No. He's a singer.

BEAN: *(Embarrassed)* Oh, Godfrey… Is he good?

NEWT: Man's got the best set of lungs this side of the Mississip.

BEAN: You sing?

NEWT: No ma'am. I can plucka mean banjo, though.

BEAN: You can?

NEWT: Some folks up North say I got the trickiest fingers in seven

counties.

BEAN: I'll bet if you had yourself a banjo you'd start pluckin it straight away.

NEWT: I might.

BEAN: Really?

NEWT: I might indeed.

BEAN: You would, just like that! I can tell!

NEWT: You can?

BEAN: Yessir, I can.

NEWT: And how's that?

BEAN: Just by the way your settin there. Like you got certain thorts. Like you're thinkin on that Barcelona chair. I mean you might, right?

NEWT: I might, indeed.

BEAN: I had a feelin!

NEWT: And then again, I might just ask you to dance with me instead.

BEAN: You wouldn't.

NEWT: On top of old smoky, Bean. If my wheel was workin I'd knucklestep it for a throw or two.

BEAN: Ain't seen nary a knucklestep afore.

NEWT: Thing about knucklesteppin is it ain't like dancin regular.

BEAN: What's it like?

NEWT: Well, you start out dancin regular. A tripletime with some boot slappin and such. But then it turns wild and furious. You throw your elbows out and start flappin like a rooster. And you dip kinda low like you're drinkin water from a trough and then you pop back up, still flappin them wings.

BEAN: *(Excited)* You are fibbin to me Newton Yardly.

NEWT: You get a coupla seasoned knucklesteppers at a barn jamboree and a man who knows somethin about a fiddle, and I'll tell you so many folks'll get up and start dancin you'd think religious thoughts.

BEAN: Sounds crazy.

NEWT: Crazy fun.

BEAN: All them folks doin that!

NEWT: Some of the best knucklesteppers I know travel from county to county. Just dance in barns and get folks to join in. That's all they do.

BEAN: But why do they call it knucklesteppin if it ain't got nothin to do with no knuckles?

NEWT: Cause if you do it right your knuckles will pearl up and you'll feel like you got sodapop coarsin through your veins.

BEAN: Sodypop!

(NEWT *demonstrates the wing-flapping in his chair, his knuckles facing out. He does this for a moment and then bursts into laughter.* BEAN *laughs, too. Then she tries and then they both flap their arms simultaneously. The laughter subsides.)*

BEAN: I used to play the saw.

NEWT: You don't say.

BEAN: Could make it sound like a nightdog bellerin. *(She mimes playing the saw and sings softly for a few moments.)*

NEWT: Well, that's an awful pretty sound, Bean.

(BEAN waves NEWT off, embarrassed.)

NEWT: Where is it?

BEAN: What.

NEWT: Your saw.

BEAN: Oh, it's gone. *(Referring to the tabletop)* Swapped it to the tinker for this door.

NEWT: Good old tinker.

(Pause)

BEAN: Can I ask you somethin, Mister Newton Yardly?

NEWT: You may.

BEAN: You still got all your teeth?

NEWT: Every last one of em. Some of em don't work so hot, but I can still tear up a sticka jerky if I'm in the right frame of mind. Why do you ask?

BEAN: Oh, I don't know. Just think folks ort to keep all their teeth, that's all.

NEWT: You still got all yours?

BEAN: All cep one.

NEWT: It broke on you?

BEAN: Went rotten. I pulled it out with a table wrench.

NEWT: Did it hurt?

BEAN: Not really. Stank, though.

NEWT: I reckon it did.

BEAN: Smelled like blue toe.

NEWT: Blue toe!

(BEAN *and* NEWT *share laughter. The laughter dies.*)

BEAN: I can't read… And I ain't been outside in a dog's age. Oh, I'll look out the window once in a while. See a switchmouse settin up. Tiny little thing. Small as a thumbfinger. Bushchickens trottin by. Lookin at you like they wanna say somethin. Their funny little heads. Once I even saw a five foot turkeybird dancin like a man. Jigdancin on a stump. Five feet tall. Trickyhop jimstep keep em all in line. Feathers all fanned out. Colors that don't even have names. Just dancin there. All five feet of him.

Once in a while I'll even open the door and stand there for a moment. Just to smell the air. The trees. The rain. A smokefire. Folks strollin through the woods. The way the clouds change up and get that stink of shelf iron.

But I like it in here. I got my Life Room. My feedin table. My clothes weaver. My cookstove. My pots and pans. Utensils and such…

NEWT: What if you had to?

BEAN: Had to?

NEWT: Leave the house. What if one of them mudslops was on and the house started slidin and you didn't have time to get roped in.

BEAN: But them bushchickens would be goin backwards and I'd see em.

NEWT: But what if you didn't. Hypothetically speakin, of course.

BEAN: What's that?

NEWT: What's what?

BEAN: Hypo… thel…

NEWT: Just pretend speakin. What would you do?

(*Beat*)

BEAN: I know secrets about food that you won't never find in nary a recipe book. And I can handle a shovelaxe better than most men.

NEWT: I learned how to read when I was in the service. Started me out on the bible.

BEAN: Did you like it?

NEWT: No. Not really. Some pretty good stuff on revenge, though.
Interestin folks in that book. Jesus. Job. Jacob. Santa Clause.

BEAN: Santy Clause ain't in nary a bible story.

NEWT: Sure he is.

BEAN: That's crazy.

NEWT: There's one story where they got him and Jesus shootin dice.

BEAN: Like fun there is.

NEWT: Old Fat Santy and Jesus Christola himself. Slingin craps right in Jerusalem… *Snake eyes!*

BEAN: Oh that's just outrageous!

(BEAN *and* NEWT *share laughter.*)

(POINTER *peers in through the window. He watches* BEAN *and* NEWT, *undetected.*)

NEWT: Rayanne, I must say that you have the prettiest hair I've seen in a long time.

BEAN: *(Feeling her hair self-consciously)* Oh Newton Yardly that's hog gravy.

NEWT: Not hog gravy at all. As pretty a batch I've seen in a long time. Blackberry brown. And you got that streak goin. Color of wheatfire. You ever seen a field of wheat catch fire?

BEAN: Can't say that I have.

NEWT: One of the purest golds you'll ever see. Golder than gold.

(BEAN *continues to cover her hair.*)

NEWT: Now don't go blockin it on me.

BEAN: You're just sayin stuff like that cause you're two-thirds in shock.

NEWT: That hair of yours is liable to take a man directly outta shock.

BEAN: Ain't you supposed to be hurt?

NEWT: Nothin some fine company and a good batcha whiskey couldn't touch.

BEAN: Would you like some more Newton Yardly?

NEWT: I think I would.

(BEAN *rises, crosses to the door, removes a Hefty bag poncho from a hook by the door, puts it on.*)

BEAN: I'll be right back.

(BEAN *exits the house very slowly, as though she is walking into a dark room. The sound of wind and rain again.*)

(NEWT *reaches into his vest, removes a large automatic German handgun. He releases the magazine, checks it, pushes it back in, places it on his lap, covers his lap with the blanket.* POINTER *disappears from the window.*)

(BEAN *reenters with an old container of Tide liquid detergent. Her hair is wet. She closes the door and removes her poncho, placing it back on the hook. She crosses to* NEWT, *hands him the container, standing near him now.*)

BEAN: Special batch. Been savin it.

NEWT: Smells like honeysuckle… Honeysuckle drink. Apple hair.

BEAN: I thort you said my hair was like blackberries.

NEWT: It's the color of blackberries but it smells like apples.

(*Suddenly,* POINTER *enters wielding a makeshift crossbow.*)

POINTER: Get away from that man, Momma.

BEAN: Pointer, you put that down this instant!

NEWT: (*Arms in the air*) I'd advise you to put that thing down.

POINTER: Mister, you don't know me from a can of grease! You got no business callin me your son!

NEWT: I never called you son.

BEAN: Pointer, you have gone entirely out of your mind!

POINTER: Move away from him, Momma!

BEAN: I will do nary the thing!

POINTER: This man's got a gun, Momma! A pistola! I just saw him loadin it a minute ago! It's on his lap!

BEAN: The only thing this man's got is a belly fulla whiskey and a wound on his leg!

POINTER: Pull that quilt off his lap.

BEAN: How can you be such a fool!

POINTER: Lift up the blanket, Momma! See for yourself!

(BEAN *approaches him slowly.*)

POINTER: If he so much as flinches…

(BEAN *lifts the blanket. The handgun rests on his lap.*)

POINTER: Now Momma, we're gonna be careful as kittens in a snow storm. I want you to grab the pistola off his lap and come on over here by me. (*To* NEWT) Mister, keep them sticks high. And don't even think about creepin up behind me!

NEWT: I ain't goin nowhere. I'm stayin right here.

POINTER: Don't you dare think about creepin up behind me!

(BEAN *removes the pistol puts it in her bra, crosses to* POINTER, *seizes the crossbow, aims it at* NEWT *with authority.*)

NEWT: *(To* BEAN*)* Like I told you, I was passin through and my truck clutched up on me and I was cuttin through the woods—

POINTER: That's so much horsecrap it's startin to smell like a stable in here.
No one comes through these parts with no vehicle no more!

NEWT: Son, that's the long and the short of it.

POINTER: I done told you about that son business!

NEWT: Please. I'm tellin you the truth.

BEAN: *(Referring to the gun in her bra)* Then, what was you plannin on doin with this gun?

NEWT: I wasn't plannin nothin. Somethin crazy's goin on out there, that's all. Some fool's runnin around takin duckshots at folks. I just wanted to be ready in case he crawled in through the window.

POINTER: So why'd you have to hide it under that quilt then?

BEAN: Thort you was gonna throw that over your shoulders.

NEWT: My leg got cold. I was, but my leg started freezin up on me.

POINTER: Why couldn't you show it to my Momma?

NEWT: I didn't want to scare her. I was just tryin to *protect* your mother.

POINTER: Well she don't need no protectin. We do fine by ourselves, don't we, *Rayanne*?

BEAN: Pointer, why don't you go over there and see if he's got a wallet.

NEWT: *(To* POINTER*)* Inside pocket of my vest.

(POINTER *crosses to* NEWT, *finds his wallet, moves away.)*

BEAN: He got any I D?

POINTER: No.

NEWT: I'm Newt. Newton Yardly from Jackson County. My daddy's name was Newton Yardly and his daddy's name was Newton Yardly. Straight on down the line.

BEAN: You been lyin to me this whole time.

NEWT: I'm tellin you I was just tryin to protect folks.

BEAN: There's only one thing I hate more than a liar, and that's a liar with a sweet voice.

NEWT: Ma'am, I been walloped in the leg—

BEAN: Comin in here talkin about your truck and gettin shot and struck by lightnin--

NEWT: Those ain't lies. Those are real things that happened to me. Real as water.

BEAN: Just settin up in my Life Room. Drinking my whiskey. Bleedin all over my floor, talkin about knucklesteppin and all that. Playin word games. I'm just tryin to do right by helpin a citizen out. You do that and the good lord knows it comes back to you. But when it happens like this it feels like somethin has shifted wrong. Tell him to get up, Pointer.

POINTER: Get up!

NEWT: Hey now young fella—

POINTER: I said get up!

(NEWT *stands. He groans in pain, clutching his leg.)*

BEAN: Outside.

(NEWT *hobbles to the door.)*

BEAN: *(To* POINTER*)* Get the door.

*(*POINTER *opens the door.* BEAN *pushes* NEWT *outside with the crossbow. As soon as he is outside she hands the crossbow to* POINTER*. He exits with it, closing the door.)*

(After they are outside, BEAN *walks over to the electricity area, near the generator bike, seizes an extension cord, crosses with it to the table, pours herself a drink.)*

(From outside, an audible thwunk! Is heard, then NEWT*'s voice screaming in pain.)*

(Moments later, POINTER *enters, pushing* NEWT *in front of him, prodding him with the emptied crossbow. There is an arrow sticking out of* NEWT*'s leg, just above the knee.* POINTER *pushes* NEWT *to the floor.* NEWT *is still screaming, in severe pain.* NEWT *limps absurdly, clutching the same, splinted leg.* POINTER *sets the crossbow down.)*

NEWT: Same leg! Same leg! God awmighty!

*(*NEWT *He reaches out to* BEAN *for the new container of whiskey, but she refuses it.)*

POINTER: *(Grabbing the protruding arrow, twisting)* Now, you better tell us what your business is, or I'm gonna start gettin fancy!

NEWT: *(Barely able to get it out)* Jesus God.

POINTER: Let me check if they're here. Jesus?! God!? You hidin in here somewhere? How bout Santy Clause? Santy, you up there on the roof? Maybe he's shootin some craps. I guess not.

NEWT: *(Gasping)* Oh my god I think my knee's missin.

POINTER: *(Mocking)* Oh my god I think my knee's missin. *(He moves to twist the arrow again.)*

NEWT: I didn't come to collect! Didn't come for that!

POINTER: WELL THEN WHAT THE HELL YOU COME FOR!

NEWT: *(Starting to fade)* I came for Jeff… Folks hired me. Four days ago.

POINTER: No one knew he was gettin out of Shiloh tonight! Nary a soul knew bout that!

NEWT: On the inside. They knew. Folks know everything on the inside.
He killed a man. Important man. They hired me… He killed a man. With his bare hands. Said he used his thumbs. Drove his thumbs. Clear through. Drove em clear through.

POINTER: Clear through what!

NEWT: His eyes… A bounty. They hired me… They put a bounty on his head.

(BEAN *rises with extension cord, which is pulled taught, wrapped around her fists. She approaches* NEWT, *wraps it around* NEWT's *neck, and strangles him until he is dead. This will take a great effort. He whispers, Please, please, please," pleading for his life, but to no avail. After he is thoroughly dispatched she puts his handgun back in his pocket.)*

(POINTER *crosses to the car trunk and removes a hatchet. He crosses back to* NEWT, *starts to measure him up at the back of the neck.)*

(POINTER *raises the hatchet. A girl's voice)*

SHIRLEY: *(Off)* Hello?

(POINTER *freezes.* BEAN *and* POINTER *look at each other, then proceed to drag* NEWT *to the upstage left corner. They prop him up, put a hat on his head, pull the brim down over his eyes, push his knee up, places his hand on his knee, open his mouth, arrange a cigarette in it.)*

SHIRLEY: *(Off)* Pointer Scully are you home? … Pointer O'Daniel Scully …I gotta talk to you!

(POINTER *opens the door.* SHIRLEY JUDYHOUSE *stands in the entrance, soaked from the rain, holding a pie tin and carrying a suitcase. She is frantic, out of breath, exhilarated. She wears a summer dress. Rainwater runs down her arms, which are infested with the same sores that* POINTER *has. It appears that the pie tin has been shot through the center. The contents of the pie have exploded all over the front of her dress.*)

(POINTER *approaches her cautiously, as though she is some sacred object. He takes her suitcase, places it down.*)

SHIRLEY: Hello Mrs Scully. I'm Shirley Judyhouse. I brought you a shoofly pie, but I think it got struck by lightning. I'm an awful mess. I'm so sorry.

(BEAN *pours herself a glass of whiskey from the Tide container.*)

SHIRLEY: Y'all were fixin to have dinner, weren't you?

(BEAN *studies her.*)

SHIRLEY: I'm sorry I barged in on you like this. I just walked two miles in the flash rain. Figured I'd save some time by cuttin through the woods. Them woods was throwin fluff last night. Looked like snow was fallin. But the flash rain's turned it all into a slopyard. Looks like corn porridge all over the ground. They say the mudslop's comin.

I made the pie myself. Three cups of molasses, half a cup of brown sugar, quarter cup of shortenin. Let it brown slightly and presto-change-o you got yourself a shoofly pie. Pointer always tells me how much he likes the smell of molasses. My Momma says if there's one way to reach a man it's through your pie.

(POINTER *removes his T-shirt, begins drying* SHIRLEY *with it, bare-chested now.*)

SHIRLEY: I know it looks more like a trainwreck, but that's cause of the storm. I was runnin through the

woods and all of the sudden the sky opened up and
the flash rain went white and I heard this *explosion*.
Sounded like a tree snappin in half. Next thing I
know, my pie's been struck by lightning! Ain't that the
craziest thing? I had to pick it up off the ground. I was
so scared I started countin. My momma always said
that if you count fast enough it'll keep ghosts away.
So I started countin as fast as I could. I got clear up to
five hundred and forty-seven by the time I got to your
door. Five-forty-seven... Oh my god, there is a man
chillin' in the corner and he's bleedin like a scalped
chicken!

(*An awkward pause*)

SHIRLEY: Well, anyway, I made it. Here I am.

BEAN: Here you are.

(SHIRLEY *covers her mouth suddenly.*)

SHIRLEY: Pointer, would you be so kind as to direct me
to the whereabouts of the nearest lavatory? I think I'm
gonna be sick.

(POINTER *leads* SHIRLEY *outside, re-enters a moment later.*)

BEAN: So that's Little Miss Judyhouse.

(POINTER *nods.*)

BEAN: The one and only.

(POINTER *nods.*)

BEAN: The famous head licker.

(*From off, sounds of* SHIRLEY *vomiting.* BEAN *smokes,
exhales.*)

BEAN: I hope she's got a accordion in that suitcase,
cause I'll eat the nails out the floorboards if she thinks
she's stayin.

POINTER: She's real smart, Momma. She's the one
who's been teachin me how to read.

BEAN: You don't *know* how to read! We ain't the readin type! And no skinny little dipstick is gonna come into my Life Room and start battin around her sinful, ingenerate eyelashes and expect to get away with it!

(SHIRLEY *re-enters, wiping her mouth.*)

SHIRLEY: I don't think ingenerate is a word, Missus Scully. But *de*generate is a word.

(BEAN *is quietly furious.*)

SHIRLEY: I could teach you to read, Missus Scully. Pointer told me how you can't read. I taught Pointer how to read, didn't I Pointer?
It's simple as bubble gum once you learn the alphabet. And then you learn about vowels and consonants and syllibiscuits I mean syllables. But first you gotta start with your A B Cs.

BEAN: You will teach me no such thing! Readin don't make nary a difference!

SHIRLEY: Ain't no need to yell, Missus Scully.

BEAN: Who the hell do you think you're talkin to?!

SHIRLEY: (*Guarding her stomach*) I'm with child, Missus Scully! You shouldn't yell, it'll upset the Biggity-biggity-baby!

(*An awkward pause.* POINTER *attempts to exit the house, but* SHIRLEY *gently grabs him by the back of his shorts.*)

SHIRLEY: I'm gonna have a baby and it's gonna have long legs and crazy eyes.

BEAN: Oh, for the fun of Jesus.

SHIRLEY: And when it grows up it's gonna be a first-class freestylin emcee battle champion, just like its daddy.

POINTER: Oh, for the fun of Jesus.

(SHIRLEY *takes* POINTER's *hands, places them on her stomach.*)

SHIRLEY: Feel how warm my belly is, Pointer? It's like somethin's cookin in there, ain't it? *(To* BEAN*)* Missus Scully, Pointer and I are lovers of the most devastatin degree. And I intend on marryin him and raisin our baby together.

BEAN: You mind tellin me how this happened?

SHIRLEY: It all starts with a little bee buzzin around a flower, Missus Scully.
Then the summer breeze just makes things ripe and somethin sweet gets in the air, and fish start swimmin backwards and dogs start howlin, and the firechief starts invitin folks over to the firehouse, and love starts flowin like that slow July breeze.

(SHIRLEY *holds both of* POINTER's *hands tenderly, looks intently into his eyes.*)

SHIRLEY: I knew the minute I laid eyes on Pointer that we would forge a union of bewildering desire and violet passion. He was settin up in a tree on Denorfia Memorial Boulevard and I saw that head glowing in the twilight and those long skinny legs danglin over the branches. You coulda hit me with a skillet and I wouldn'ta known the difference. My momma says that kinda feelin don't come by but once. We been meetin each other nearly every day down by the fishpond, haven't we, Pointer? He's told me stuff he ain't never told no one. Thoughts that he has. His philosophy on Hip-hop Music. How bein sexy ain't nothin more than a walk and a talk and a way of settin in a chair. He's told me true stories, too. Like about what his daddy did to him and how he died and how you always go around tellin folks he fell into a hole. And how you're afraid to go outside. I know about all that, Missus Scully. It don't matter to me. I love Pointer anyways.

We pledge our love with johnson grass. And sometimes we go skinny dippin. And the troutfish swim under our private parts. And sometimes we'll climb up in a tree and eat leaves. One day we ate thirty-four leaves. We fed em to each other, back and forth. Just like Adam and Eve musta done. That's when we did it. Right on the branch of that tree. That's when we made our baby, ain't it Pointer?

And every day I can feel it growin in me. At first I pitchered it like a baby chick. All blond and soft. Then I started seein it like a little fluffy kitten. I would sing to it and meow. And sometimes I would pretend like it was meowin back at me. Then it turned into a puppy with floppy ears. And now it's a baby horse. A tiny one. Smaller than a fist. And soon it'll be a little Pointer in my stomach. With a beautiful vanilla-butterscotch bald head and big baggy basketball shorts. And I'll play classic hip-hop ceedees every night before I go to bed. Jungle Brothers. Black Sheep. De la Soul. Poor Righteous Teachers. And I'll feel my baby's smile ticklin the inside of my belly. A little Pointer. Even if it's a girl I know it'll come out to be just like Pointer. I'll just name her Pointy.

(SHIRLEY *takes* POINTER *by the hand and leads him to the center of the dining room. She suddenly starts to sing in a high, melodious voice.* SHIRLEY *and* POINTER *begin to slow dance during the song.* BEAN *looks on. As they dance,* SHIRLEY *steps onto* POINTER's *Timberlands.)*

SHIRLEY: *(Singing)*
For every flower
There's a summer song
and it floats up
to the trees

For every desert
There's a water pond

where a drink
is drunk for free

For every rowboat
There's a fisherman
who cries
into the sea

And all my nights
I dream of daffodils
cause I know
you're here with me.

(Suddenly, from under the house, the sound of desperate hacking. POINTER *and* SHIRLEY *stop dancing and stare at the floor. More hacking, and then a moment later, wood slowly cracking. A muddy hand. A muddy arm. Another muddy hand bursts through the floorboards, holding a shovelaxe, caked in mud and clay. Arms reaching out. Then a bald, mud-slogged head. Then shoulders.* JEFF *pushes himself up into the Life Room. In an orange penitentiary jumpsuit he is completely covered with mud, from head to toe. The thirty-aught-six is strapped around his shoulder. After he pulls himself out of the hole he kneels on the floor, breathing intensely. It is as if he has dug through the center of the earth.)*

BEAN: Jeff.

*(*BEAN *slowly approaches* JEFF, *as does* POINTER. *They hug him. He hugs* POINTER, *lifeless somehow.* POINTER *takes the rifle and the shovel and sets them in the corner. After a moment,* JEFF *gets to his feet, standing wobbly. He looks around the room, taking things in. He slowly crosses to his place at the table. The others watch intently.)*

*(*JEFF *slowly sits and starts to eat. He eats slowly at first, and then faster and faster. It quickly devolves into an animal, desperate storm of consumption.* BEAN *rises and helps to serve him enormous helpings, which he shovels into his mouth, pawing at the food like a starved beast. At some point*

she hands a bowl to pointer, he places it on the makeshift stove for reheating, mans the dynamo wheel, hand-pedaling, increasing the electricity in the house. He eats ravenously, consuming almost everything on the table.)

(After JEFF finishes, he simply stares down at the table, catatonic. BEAN nods to POINTER. POINTER exits. BEAN crosses to JEFF, starts to clean JEFF's face with a rag.)

SHIRLEY: That was one of the most amazin things I've ever seen. My daddy don't even eat like that and he's huge!

BEAN: You ort to get up a minute and walk around. Let it take to you.

(JEFF stares out blankly.)

BEAN: Your face changed just the way I thort.

(BEAN washes his mouth, his ears, around his eyes. There is a large blue spot around his eye. When she cleans his neck area, a large scar appears.)

SHIRLEY: *(Crossing to JEFF, going to her knees)* A scar!

BEAN: Oh my Godfrey.

SHIRLEY: A real scar! *(She touches the scar, follows it with her finger.)* It's like a smile.

BEAN: They cut my boy. They cut my sweet, sweet boy.

(POINTER re-enters carrying a small, feeble-looking tree behind him. He sets it near the table.)

BEAN: Look what they done to him, Pointer.

SHIRLEY: They tried to cut him like a chicken!

(They all watch JEFF, who is captivated by the tree. He crosses to it, touches it tenderly, smells it.)

BEAN: It's a present from Pointer, Jeff.

POINTER: I been growin it for you.

BEAN: We're gonna plant it in the ground. Right in front of the house. And when it gets thick enough he's gonna climb it and set in it.

POINTER: Figure some birds might want to nest in it, too. Some jaybirds or somethin.

SHIRLEY: I like jaybirds. Sometimes they'll set right outside the ledge of our kitchen window. I like talkin to em. I'll say "hey little jaybird." Oh, they're just the fanciest things.

(JEFF *beckons* SHIRLEY. *She goes to him. He whispers into her ear.*)

BEAN: What'd he say?

SHIRLEY: He said, "It's a tree".

POINTER: He can speak?

(JEFF *shakes his head, whispers into* SHIRLEY'*s ear.*)

SHIRLEY: He said he can only make little whispers.

POINTER: You can name it, Jeff. It don't have a name yet.

(JEFF *picks three leaves off the tree, puts them in the pocket of his orange jumpsuit, then whispers in* SHIRLEY'*s ear.*)

SHIRLEY: He said they tried to cut him.

(JEFF *whispers into* SHIRLEY'*s ear.*)

SHIRLEY: He said they tried to take his voice away.

BEAN: You've grown right up into a man.

(BEAN *hugs* JEFF, *he breaks the hug, whispers into* SHIRLEY'*s ear.*)

SHIRLEY: He said they took his voice away, but it's starting to come back…You can cut a throat and take the voice, but if the throat is good it grows back.

BEAN: (*Simply*) I had a dream about this. I dreamed you was walkin in some crops. Some barley or wheatstick…

I knew it was you cause I could smell you. You was just walkin along. It was night and the moon was big as a whale's heart. Lookeded like you was gonna walk right into it and get swallowed up. I was chasin after you and callin your name but you couldn't hear me so I kept on after you.

When I caught up to you I tapped you on your shoulder. And you turnt around, but afore I could say anything you changed into Pointer. You turnt skinny and you went paler. But you still smelt like you. And then you started walkin again.

And the crops got higher and them wheatsticks changed into sweetcorn, tall as my waist. Them stalks was pressin up on me. But I fought em. I used my arms and I used my hands and I used the harvestin skills I learnt when I was a girlie.

And I started closin in on you. I could reach out and almost touch you. Could almost put my hand on your head. Then I did. I catched you. So I tapped you on the shoulder again, but when you turnt around this time, you wasn't Pointer no more. You was a stranger—

(JEFF *whispers into* SHIRLEY's *ear.*)

SHIRLEY: He said he wants to call it Daddytree.

BEAN: You don't wanna call it that, Jeff. There are plenty of other things you could call it.

(JEFF *whispers into* SHIRLEY's *ear.*)

SHIRLEY: He said that Daddytree is perfect. Perfect as puppy piss.

(JEFF *whispers more into* SHIRLEY's *ear.*)

SHIRLEY: He said he figures his Daddy's buried deep in the mud somewhere around here, so he wants to make it his tree.

(JEFF *whispers more into* SHIRLEY's *ear.*)

SHIRLEY: He said maybe his daddy'll snatch on to them roots and come out new. And maybe someday Pointer'll come back home and he'll see Daddy up there in them branches with some jaybirds and he'll be different.

BEAN: Pointer ain't goin nowhere.

(JEFF *grabs* SHIRLEY *quickly, firmly, whispers into her ear.*)

SHIRLEY: He said yes he is.

BEAN: He's stayin right here. Right here with us.

(JEFF *whispers more into* SHIRLEY'*s ear.*)

SHIRLEY: He said Pointer's gonna go to a big city and become a first-class emcee battle champion. He said he's got enough lyrics to start a thunderstorm. He said he knows cause of all the letters he's gotten from him… He said that Pointer will come home some day and his daddy'll be right up there in them branches and he won't never hurt him again… Cause he won't ever be able to leave that tree. Cause he'll be part of it… Instead of bones he'll have sticks. And instead of blood he'll have maple syrup. He'll have to build a tree house and (*Pointing to* BEAN) you'll have to bring his food up to him. And if he leaves his house he'll die. He'll die twice.

(JEFF *crosses to the hole, reaches into it, removes a canvas duffel bag slogged in mud. From it he produces an enormous manuscript, almost two feet thick. He lets it drop on the floor.* SHIRLEY *crosses to the manuscript, kneels down to read it.*)

SHIRLEY: (*Reading the title page*) "Two-Thousand, One-Hundred and Thirty-Eight Sandwiches"

BEAN: (*To* JEFF) You wrote that?

(JEFF *nods.*)

SHIRLEY: *(Shuffling through it)* It's two thousand one hundred and thirty-eight pages long! *(She turns to the Foreword. Reading)* "Foreword: Two-Thousand, One-Hundred and Thirty-Eight Sandwiches by Jeffrey Catilla Scully.

"I have been locked up two-thousand one hundred and thirty-eight days. This book is a log of those days and it is dedicated to my mother, Rayanne Scully.

"While at Shiloh State Penitentiary, where I have been incarcerated for killing my father, who was in the process of defiling my only brother, I wrote about a different sandwich every day.

"'Every night after lights out I would set up in bed and think up a new one. I used different meats and cheeses. Breads. Ketchups and mustards. Every combination imaginable. Fish sandwiches. Meat sandwiches. Jelly sandwiches. Peanut butter sandwiches. Sandwiches that are toasted. Sandwiches with layers. All sorts of sandwiches. I invented stuff. As you will see, there is even a sandwich with some Duracell batteries in it.

"My writing technique was this: I would compose the sandwiches on two separate pieces of paper. I would put one of them in the book and I would eat the other one. I would crumple it up and pop it in my mouth and close my eyes, and in my mind I would picture that sandwich. The ingredients. The sauces. The texture of the bread. And it would be like I was eating the real thing. Like it was sliding right down my gullet.

"I hope you enjoy this, Mother Scully, as I was the one who had to endure such a difficult season of my life, and I have suffered innumerable lost days on your behalf. All these sandwiches are for you."

(JEFF kneels down beside SHIRLEY, whispers into her ear.)

SHIRLEY: *(To BEAN)* He said he wants you to come outside with him for a minute.

(Awkward pause. JEFF *whispers more.)*

SHIRLEY: *(To* BEAN*)* He said it'll just take a minute. Just you and him.

POINTER: But she don't go outside, Jeff.

*(*JEFF *whispers into* SHIRLEY's *ear.)*

SHIRLEY: He said he saw her out there earlier… Carryin some Tide.

BEAN: Why do you want me to go outside, Jeffrey?

*(*JEFF *whispers into* SHIRLEY's *ear.)*

SHIRLEY: *(To* POINTER*)* He said he made somethin else for her.

BEAN: What is it?

*(*JEFF *whispers into* SHIRLEY's *ear.)*

SHIRLEY: He said it's a hole.

BEAN: A hole?

SHIRLEY: *(To* BEAN*)* He said he he dug it up special for you.

*(*JEFF *whispers into* SHIRLEY's *ear.)*

SHIRLEY: He said he really wants you to see your hole, Missus Scully.

BEAN: How bout some lemonade. You didn't drink nary a drop.

*(*BEAN *grabs the pitcher of lemonade, hands it to* JEFF. *He holds it for a moment, then pours half of it into the base of the tree.)*

POINTER: We could plant your tree in that hole, Jeff.

*(*JEFF *whispers to* SHIRLEY.*)*

SHIRLEY: He said that wouldn't work.

BEAN: Why not?

*(*JEFF *whispers to* SHIRLEY.*)*

SHIRLEY: ...Because it goes against the Laws of Nature.

(JEFF *whispers more.*)

SHIRLEY: He said that when you dig up a hole you have to feed it. You have to feed a hole before it'll grow anything.

BEAN: Then take that body over there.

(JEFF *whispers to* SHIRLEY.)

SHIRLEY: ...He said that won't work.

BEAN: Why not?

(JEFF *whispers to* SHIRLEY.)

SHIRLEY: He said cause it's dead. Can't feed no dead body to a hole. Hole won't take to it.

NEWT: (*Suddenly alive*) Hotfoot showdown...lookin for a throwdown...don't believe that burger...he from the nowhere no town. (*He makes a sound like* BEAN's *saw noise from earlier, then dies again.*)

(JEFF *whispers more to* SHIRLEY.)

SHIRLEY: He said a hole gets hungry when there's nothin in it...

(JEFF *whispers more to* SHIRLEY.)

SHIRLEY: And that if you dip low enough you can hear it breathin.

(JEFF *whispers to* SHIRLEY.)

SHIRLEY: (*To* BEAN) He said it'll only take but a minute, Missus Scully.

BEAN: (*To* JEFF, *falling to her knees*) Why won't you talk to me! I'm standin right here in front of you! I ain't no ghost!

(JEFF *whispers more to* SHIRLEY.)

SHIRLEY: He said once we get it fed, we can plant the tree. *(To* POINTER*)* Then when you come home to visit you can drop some mad hellified lyrics in front of it.

*(*JEFF *reaches into his pocket, produces a folded piece of paper, crosses to* POINTER, *hands it to him.* POINTER *accepts it.* JEFF *gestures to* POINTER *to read from the piece of paper.* POINTER *does so. He has to work some of the words out, as he is clearly an early reader.* SHIRLEY *might help him with a word or two.)*

POINTER: *(Reading from the piece of paper)*
Some folks got a history in their family.
A smell in their home.
A music in their voices.
Songs are sung by fires.
I seen it.
I seen all that stuff.
I used to sneak into a house.
Sneak in like a spirit.

*(*SHIRLEY *helps* POINTER *pronounce "spirit".)*

POINTER:
Like I was some tree shade creepin on the floor.
Just to watch them sleep.
Just to watch the moon on their face.
Cause the moon will set on a face and make it look real nice.
Real nice.
Like there's a gladness inside.

*(*SHIRLEY *helps* POINTER *pronounce "gladness".)*

*(*JEFF *starts to move toward* BEAN. *Just as he is about to grab her,* POINTER *starts to perform the rap he'd been writing for* JEFF's *return. He loses his speech impediment entirely. It is fast and impressive and altogether a new side of* POINTER.*)*

(Pointer's Funky Joint)

POINTER: Tatter-da-malion
Yo I'm feelin crazy man
Yo you made me understand
What its like to be a man.
Dealin with the silence
Digging holes a science
Dealin with the nightmares
Makin due with violence.
Man I feel like cryin
I hear them frogs a sighin
The trees they keep on creaking
Even though they dyin.
Tinkers selling sody-pop
Bopping through the mudslop
Every summer picking crops
When they grow they never stop.
This house is like a freestyle
Everything we found
What I was as a child: buried in the ground
Mama says I'm actin wild
Cause my head is round
Them sounds of them hounds comin
echoes all a round.
Chillin in the slippin zone
Not even half grown
We don't got no telephone
We don't got no dial tone
But my mouths a megaphone
I use it like a microphone
Cause I know I'm not alone
Sittin on this tombstone…
Yea, I got my brothers bones, fillin up my SOUL
Waiting for my bloodman up at shilOH.
Daddy was a scully man, he fell down a hole
I done wanna get m'self back what daddy stole.
I used to be a bed wetter till I got your letters
Made me feel real better throwing off my fetters.

I feel like a bird Jeff
Sitting in the trees
It used to be four Jeff
But now it's only three.
I've never felt free
And death don't phase me
But two aint enough to have a fam-i-ly
You see?
Thank god for Jay-Z!
Aint no soda –bush- rope gonna save me *(2x)*
Only BLOOD brother gonna give me what I need
Only BLOOD brother gonna give me li-ber-ty.
My heart burned like homebrew when I thought of you
(2x)

*(*NEWT'*s cell phone rings.* JEFF *reaches in* NEWT'*s pockets, removes the phone, answers it. He speaks audibly for the first time, but the sound produced is strange, dislocated, raw.)*

JEFF: Hello?... Yes, this is he... We got him, yeah... That's confirmed, yes... About an hour ago... Okay...

*(*JEFF *hangs up. He falls to his knees, exhausting almost everything he has in reserve, having had to speak. He pushes himself off the floor, strips his penitentiary clothes off, standing naked before the others for a moment. The story of prison is told on his body. Wounds. Tattoos. Brutalized flesh)*

JEFF: I'm not a man no more.
I'm a clicking cat.
A clicking cat man.
I'm growin a tail.
And I got a mouse for a heart.
A mouse I swallowed six years ago.

(Another man, GORDON, *emerges from the hole in the floor. He is also slogged with mud, drenched from the storm. Like* JEFF, *he is wearing orange penitentiary clothes, and his head is crudely shaved, and there is a blue spot tattooed around*

his eye. Somehow his jaw has been wired shut with a coat hanger. There is a small tin funnel hanging around his neck like a strange necklace.)

(GORDON gets to his feet, nods to JEFF. JEFF returns the nod. He makes several clicking noises with his tongue and mouth. JEFF responds with his own clicking noises. It is clearly their exclusive, private language.)

SHIRLEY: Hello.

(GORDON springs to the table, jumping onto it like an animal, seizes the remains of every dish, every bowl, the shoofly pie, etc.)

(JEFF quickly crosses to NEWT, proceeds to strip NEWT of his clothes. He harvests everything he can: his shirt, his snakeskin boots, his socks, his pants, his handgun, his vest, his snakeskin boots, etc.)

(JEFF clicks to GORDON. GORDON produces a pair of vicegrips. JEFF opens NEWT's mouth, procedes to extract a gold tooth.)

(GORDON disappears under the table, emerges with a Twinkie, shoving it into his mouth, then jumps on top of the stove, eats from a pot, eyes POINTER's shoes, stops eating, jumps down, steals POINTER's shoes, throws them to JEFF. All this time, JEFF is taking what he can, stuffing his manuscript bag with supplies, clothes, tools, etc.)

(GORDON then inserts the tin funnel into his mouth, seizes the pitcher of lemonade pours it into the funnel, drinking. He collapses briefly, then slowly rises off the floor, staring at BEAN through the tree. Things grow suddenly very intense, very still.)

(GORDON clicks to JEFF. JEFF clicks back. GORDON springs at BEAN, seizes her, clears the table in a storm of dishes and silverware, throws her on the table. BEAN struggles but the MAN overwhelms her. POINTER moves to seize the rifle,

but JEFF *produces* NEWT*'s handgun, trains it on* POINTER.
POINTER *freezes, turns toward the corner.)*

(GORDON *thoroughly smells* BEAN, *her armpits, her breath,
the fronts and backs of her legs, her vagina, then reaches
under her dress, tears away her underpants, lowers his
jumpsuit and proceeds to rape her.)*

(JEFF *watches, still training the handgun on* POINTER.)

(The rape is savage and ends quickly.)

(Once GORDON *has climaxed, he collapses on* BEAN *for a
moment, makes her take care of him, then pushes himself
off of her, takes her off the table, sits her in a chair, arranges
her just right: crossing her legs, cupping her hands, placing
them on her knees, as if she it at church.* GORDON *then
removes his jumpsuit, and then gathers the other jumpsuit
belonging to* JEFF, *and deposits them both in the hole that
they had dug up through.* JEFF *gives him some clothes,
perhaps hand-me-downs he has foraged for, perhaps an item
or two from* NEWT*'s wardrobe,* POINTER*'s shoes.* GORDON
*dresses, then reaches over to the wall, takes the bowler hat,
places it on his head.)*

(They use NEWT*'s cellphone to take a picture:* JEFF *and the*
MAN *standing behind* BEAN, *who is seated in the chair, still
in shock, still arranged in the same way.)*

(JEFF *sets the manuscript on the floor, at* BEAN*'s feet.)*

(The MAN *clicks to* JEFF *and* JEFF *clicks back.* JEFF
approaches SHIRLEY, *beckons her. She stays behind*
POINTER. *The* MAN *rushes them, knocks* POINTER *to the
floor, seizes* SHIRLEY, *thrown her over his shoulder.* JEFF
slips. POINTER *scrambles for the shotgun, everyone freezes.*
POINTER *trains the rifle on* JEFF, JEFF *facing him now.*
POINTER *squeezes the trigger. An empty clicking sound
issues forth.)*

(JEFF *clicks back at* POINTER.)

(The MAN *clicks at* JEFF.)

(They exit quickly, SHIRLEY still over GORDON's shoulder.)

(POINTER slowly expires to the floor with the rifle.)

(BEAN is still seated in the chair, arranged as she was: her legs crossed, her hands on her knees.)

(There is a long silence. As if a season must pass.)

(Only the sounds of breathing)

(Only the sounds of the storm)

(After some time, the sounds of the storm subside. The light outside changes.)

(Eventually, the sounds of birds)

(POINTER rises up on his haunches, simply stares at BEAN.)

(A short while passes.)

(SHIRLEY enters. She is soaked from the rain and muddy. A thick line of blood can be seen running down the inside of her leg. She clasps her hands together as if she is holding something very, very small. Bloody yoke dribbles through her fingers. Her body shakes uncontrollably.)

SHIRLEY: It happened in a flash. They were closin in on him. It seemed like hundreds of em. Like they was ghost monkeys. Like they was climbin down, right outta the trees… And then the flash rain stopped and everything went quiet and them trees started snowin. Just like that. Big white fluffy oat snow fallin right offa them branches.
It fell out, Pointer. In little parts. It wasn't even a baby horse yet.

(POINTER crosses to her and clasps his hands over hers.)

SHIRLEY: We gotta go, Pointer.

(POINTER grabs her suitcase, crosses to the entrance, turns to BEAN. He opens his mouth to say something, but nothing comes out. He tries again, nothing. He tries again. Nothing)

(POINTER and SHIRLEY exit.)

(BEAN *remains seated at the table.*)

(*Eventually, she reaches down and grabs* JEFF's *manuscript. She sets it on the table, opens it.*)

(*She attempts to read it and then removes a page, balls it up, puts it into her mouth and starts to chew.*)

(*She chews deliberately, swallowing her grief. When she is through, she starts to tear another page.*)

(*At that moment* NEWT *lifts his head turns toward* BEAN.)

(*They stare at each other, frozen, as lights fade.*)

END OF PLAY

www.ingramcontent.com/pod-product-compliance
Lightning Source LLC
Chambersburg PA
CBHW070028110426

42741CB00034B/2678